PRAISE FOR *RECKLESS*:

"In *Reckless*, Andrea MacPherson runs her finger along the serrated edges of femininity. Drawing 'words like blood,' the poems probe the violence of inheritance—literary, sexual, historical—and masterfully conjure hard-won joy and camaraderie in its wake. The poet crafts a wild, resonant lyric that stitches together survival and pleasure, sewing up old wounds like embroidery."
—Adèle Barclay, author of *Renaissance Normcore*

"*Reckless* pierces through the onerous layers society imposes on women to get to the beating heart of what it means to be a girl, a mother, a lover, a best friend. These poems are sharp and soft, intimate and expansive, showing us the breadth of womanhood in the smallest and biggest of moments, in the words we speak and the ones we keep hidden."
—Jen Sookfong Lee, author of *The Hunger We Pass Down*

"*Reckless* is a brash collection of poems that chooses not to care what the naysayers think. These are poems of witness, of testament, of prayer even, for too many kinds of death, for living in the body of a woman in a world not built for her, for everyday heartaches too big and unwieldy to comprehend with anything but a poem. Campfire-confessional, *Reckless* spills all the tea in a rush, more than we think we should hear, with such generosity and trust. MacPherson leaves us feeling special, like we're the only bestie who was invited to listen."
—Michael V. Smith, author of *Soundtrack: A Lyric Memoir*

OTHER BOOKS BY ANDREA MACPHERSON

What We Once Believed
Ellipses
Away: Poems
Beyond the Blue
Natural Disasters
When She Was Electric

RECKLESS

ANDREA
MACPHERSON

Book*hug Press
Toronto 2025

FIRST EDITION

Library and Archives Canada Cataloguing in Publication

Title: Reckless / Andrea MacPherson.
Names: MacPherson, Andrea, [date]- author
Identifiers: Canadiana (print) 20250206005 | Canadiana (ebook) 20250206013
ISBN 9781771669450 (softcover)
ISBN 9781771669467 (EPUB)
Subjects: LCGFT: Poetry.
Classification: LCC PS8575.P465 R43 2025 | DDC C811/.6—dc23

The production of this book was made possible through the generous assistance of the Canada Council for the Arts and the Ontario Arts Council. Book*hug Press also acknowledges the support of the Government of Canada through the Canada Book Fund and the Government of Ontario through the Ontario Book Publishing Tax Credit and the Ontario Book Fund.

Canada Council for the Arts Conseil des Arts du Canada
Funded by the Government of Canada Financé par le gouvernement du Canada
Canada
ONTARIO ARTS COUNCIL CONSEIL DES ARTS DE L'ONTARIO
an Ontario government agency un organisme du gouvernement de l'Ontario
Ontario
ONTARIO CREATES

Book*hug Press acknowledges that the land on which we operate is the traditional territory of many nations, including the Mississaugas of the Credit, the Anishnabeg, the Chippewa, the Haudenosaunee, and the Wendat peoples. We recognize the enduring presence of many diverse First Nations, Inuit, and Métis peoples, and are grateful for the opportunity to meet and work on this territory.

for Serina and for Jen
for all of the things

and for Nora
for everything, all the time
for being my favourite person ever
I love you to the moon and back, Chicken
you and me forever

contents

THIS IS THE LAST TIME

RECKLESS

REPRODUCTIONS

reproductions,
or, before the pill

I

pessary, extended nursing, withdrawal

And yet three pale babies in as many years,
the last leaving her bloodless, cold,
her body giving up like a rock in a pond,
sinking.
    His next wife was more sturdy,
twenty-one children slipping from her easily,
her body remembering the last time too well.
Miscarriages and stillbirths in between:
    twenty-five long years of pregnancy,
her body ballooning, swelling, leaking,
the humiliations of the flesh too real—
blood, babies, breast milk,
the house sour with it all,
and the mattress sagging under his endless need.
Twenty-one names running together into an infinite stream,
the monotony of repetition, of washing diapers and bottles
and socks and underpants and frocks
and short pants and undershirts,
of each day mired in spit-up
and soured milk, of soggy bread
and handprints on the windowpanes,
beds crowded by bodies breathing in each other's dreams,
sicknesses.
    Never enough seats at the table
    never enough hands to soothe or offer love.

II

diaphragms, condoms, the temperature method

After her husband disappeared,
she slept alone in the alcove by the coal stove
and the icebox,
relishing in the narrow cot,
the way it only had room for her exhaustion.
Now, pleased to have only her own body; stillness.
The wants of the body too base,
too inconvenient, too predictable.
Pleasure just another word for trapped.
Her body obediently bleeds monthly
until it, too,
                        gives up.

III

Lysol douche, cervical cap, the rhythm method

Already old by thirty,
and so she hurries:
three boys in quick succession,
no time for rest, for scars to heal,
the body to mend. (*Will it ever mend?)*
Just her body turned inside out,
        pain so fresh it radiated
even when she slept; her body a betrayal.
Once, she'd been strong, certain,
hoisting milk jugs, tubs of wet laundry, crates of preserves.
Now, doubled over by the sink
after the last baby (*It has to be the last*)
her womb worn out, rubbed raw,
quick prayers for a reprieve,
        cramps in her uterus a relief.

IV

intrauterine device, sponges, spermicide

Knocked out, blissfully unconscious,
and then: a baby.
Mewling, downy, foreign. A baby.
This pain everywhere, all at once.
Looking for answers in the bottom of a teacup,
the leaves uncertain: *Travel? A stranger? Joy?*
Only sleep like mercy. Sleep like solace.
    Sleep like forgetting.
Her heartbeat strummed
    no more babies
    no more babies
    no more babies.
Sex a danger, a fault line;
easier to close her legs, forfeit pleasure.
The pattern of blood in her underpants:
    floral.
Did it count if no one witnessed it?
    Did it matter if no one named it?

what the doctor knew

That the world was an unhappy place,
and that pain did not begin or end
at conception:
it grew, or did not. Sometimes
it turned into something else entirely—
regret, sorrow, resentment.

That a starved three-month-old
was infinitely worse than the mass of cells
(shapeless and shape-shifting)
dropped into a bowl.

That washing your hands did not erase
the weight of speculum,
the memory of warm skin,
the crust of dried blood that he found later
on the inside of his wrist.

And mostly, that his title was something new,
but the act itself was not—
was as ancient as the impulse of bodies
    coming together,
as desperate, as messy.

the guilty party

They tell her about the guilt,
that it will settle like a winter cloak,
too heavy even in the coldest months.

And so she waited,
days sliding into weeks into months,
and yet it did not arrive.
Winter became spring
the sweet new hyacinth blooms,
milky pale and trembling,
and she was only happy for the lengthening of days,
the stronger shades of sunlight:
a plea, a promise.

Still, there was no beating her chest in regret, shame.
She thought, Another month.
                        She thought, Soon.
    She thought, Someday.

A year passed and she thought about the baby
she would have had by now—
imagined a boy, a head of dark hair,
mewls like a kitten or a small bird—
dreamed him to life,
but did not feel the lingering doubt,
all the things they had promised she'd feel:
no guilt, no regret, no shame.

Outside, the buds turned to blooms over and over,
drooping, too heavy with their own beauty,
and then dropped, withered.
Promised to do it all over again the next year,
and the next, and the next.
She wondered if she was required,

every winter, to pretend guilt,
or if, instead, she could be happy that the snow was gone,
revelling in the promise of those new stalks,
peeking up from the earth, hopeful.

accident: girl, age fifteen

Queen Anne's lace,
willow, date palm,
pomegranate,
pennyroyal—
so many words for the same
end:
        blood pooling
        between her legs,
        cotton panties ruined
        (thrown out in the trash,
        buried beneath
        Kleenex, candy wrappers,
        the soft, pink bits of eraser
        from her math homework).

No tears, only silence, the sharp pain
of her stomach contracting.

        (No, uterus.
        No, *womb*—a word from science class,
        the muddy drawing
        of a woman's reproductive organs.
        Fallopian tubes. Ovaries.
        Imagining them like strange,
        sad eggs.)

She does not think the word *baby*—
too foreign and too familiar at once,
wrong and sticky and sour in her mouth.
Instead, she tucks herself into bed,
imagines a lullaby her mother once sang,
her flannel nightgown crushed beneath her,
dotted with stars.

old wives' tales

Carry high, it's a girl.
Shaped like a watermelon? Girl.
Your face turns round, moonlike.
Acne, blemishes. Girl. Little girls steal your beauty.

A wedding ring swings back and forth for a girl,
heart rates soar.
Rest on your right side, away from your heart.
Eat chocolate, sweet fruits,
throw up every morning,
all for a girl.

    Girls are a curse.
                    Wish for anything but this.
    Dowries and duties and disappearances.

This is what a girl means.

This is what a girl means.

This is what a girl means.

wishing for blood

At first, the white cotton gusset of her underwear
was a relief—a reprieve
from scrubbing the red stains in the sink,
hiding the damp evidence
from her brothers' prying eyes.
She convinced herself that her growing stomach
was nothing more than too much
ice cream, sticky-sweet slices of cake,
ravenous, greedy.
She bound her breasts when they swelled,
when even the satin of her thin training bra
made her want to cry out in pain.

Bulky sweaters,
boys' overalls,
oversized sweatshirts,
faded, shapeless dresses from the Goodwill.

She prayed for an abscess, a tumour—
she'd heard about women
who discovered cancerous growths the size of grapefruits
in their cervixes,
believed there could be one in her womb.
Hoped.

They could cut cancer out.
She could lose a fallopian tube, her uterus,
had seen the slick diagrams in science class.
Those were survivable.

Pleasant Grove

based on the Huntsman case in Utah

Seven cardboard boxes
tucked away in the cold garage
between old luggage, Christmas lights, rusted shovels.

Unmarked, save for old, peeling labels,
seven cardboard boxes,
similar in weight, their edges folding under themselves.

Early spring with the air crisp,
he finally returns home, expecting anything but:
seven cardboard boxes.

Seven cardboard boxes
filled with ten years of death,
seventy fingers, seventy toes.

No proper burial, no funeral pyre,
no marker to remember them, no cold stone to mourn,
only seven cardboard boxes.

How had he never noticed them,
seven cardboard boxes,
some lined with greying dishtowels, holey blankets.

No maternity dresses, no baby showers,
no slatted cribs, no downy receiving blankets.
Seven cardboard boxes.

never again

taken from *Ms.* 1973

Until they saw the photo,
they'd believed she died in a car accident.
They had imagined the crushed metal,
the wail of an ambulance, too slow,
her eyes dutifully closed.
It had been so much easier.

But then: the grainy black-and-white police photo,
glossy in a women's magazine—
Ms., April 1973.

Nine years after her death,
the wound now fresh again,
hotly red and real.

> Her body folded over itself
> as if she'd been kneeling,
> praying, when she collapsed.
> Face hidden, but all her dark curls unspooling.
>
> Motel carpet grey,
> but the towels so white.
> Whiter than white.
> And the blood darker than black
> pooling beneath her,
> heavy, thick between her legs.

The girls could not look away.

This was not the mother they remembered.
Their mother smiled.
She pushed curls away from her face
and leaned forward to listen to them,

her breath soft on their cheeks.
Their mother was not bent and bloodied,
was not so completely, explicitly alone.

tubal ligation

When we were old enough, we scrubbed the floors.
Sometimes cooked in the kitchen, sometimes dressed the little ones
or changed filthy diapers. This, on the newly scrubbed floors.

Before us, shell-shocked soldiers;
before them, young women carrying books, attending lectures.
They called us the feeble-minded, but we were not. We were the
unwanted. Abandoned.

In the cellar rooms, they watched us behind glass.
We shivered naked, waited to be let out.
Phenobarbital, chlorpromazine, haloperidol when we wouldn't stop
crying.

And sometimes we were wheeled into the operating room on gurneys.
They said *appendix*, placed a mask over our faces, put us to sleep.
When we awoke, we looked at the scar on our bellies, touched it
gently.
Long and puckered pink, earthworm shivering.

We didn't even know where an appendix was.

conversations with the female poet

Write *domestic* and cross it out. Start again.
Kitchen, childhood, baby.
Erase. Yet these words remain once written;
paper has memory.

Try *loss. Choice. End.*
See how language has weight, heft.
        Words like *blood, womb, after,*
        words that are sticky, clinging to your tongue.

But still, you want the image of a hot kitchen,
a mug of tea that predicts the future.
Love. Impermanence. Barren.
        Are there other words?
        The ones you mean are the ones you do not write.

Perhaps you don't want to know
the difference between *terminate* and *miscarry.*
Perhaps the vagueness is enough
to keep your pen moving.

        They say, at least write something important—
        ecology, the environment,
        national identity.
        Do not write about love.
        Do not write about ovaries or choices
            or coat hangers.
        They say, Write about something worthwhile,
            if you must write at all.

mandatory examination for the modern girl

Learn the words *compromise*, *submission*, and *tend*. Understand
their definitions.
Cross out *career*. Cross out *want*. Cross out *other*.
These will be unnecessary, unless accompanied by *teacher*, *nurse*,
caregiver.
Then, you must learn to define *part-time*.
Mother, of course, is the exception.

Second will also be useful. There are many connotations.
Choose the one you prefer.

Because it's hard to be a girl,
learning everything necessary and needful:
how to plait your hair, how to button your coat,
how to say no without saying no,
how to measure hemlines with your fingertips,
how to cross a street, holding your keys
between your fingers,
how to yell *Fire!* instead of other, truer words,
how to mother, nurture, support,
how to clean a grimy floor, scrub stained T-shirts,
cook casseroles that bubble with comfort,
how to make soothing coos.

Because there are rules, and then more rules, sub-rules
that you must memorize. This is not open-book.
This is not multiple choice.
None of this is optional.

blooming

I can't do this, you say,
and we look up to the new spring sky,
the unnerving clean blue of it,
and I know we are both thinking of the spring cherry blossoms,
the way they unfurl, languid, glorious,
then drop to carpet suburban lawns,
busying streets with their tender pinkness.
                    You say, *I miss the coast.*

Years before, we swam in a cold pool,
too early in the year for real heat,
but the bright sunshine convincing us otherwise.
Later, we changed in my childhood bedroom, peeling
wet suits like a second skin,
the snap of elastic, the bite of the straps.
You did not turn your back,
confident, even then, in your new breasts,
the swell of your hips
under cherry-patterned bikini bottoms.

Now, we do not discuss your months of explicit want,
months of trying, when you confessed
your fears that something was wrong,
that there would never be a baby.
Cold months, our mouths pressed close
to the phone, listening, soothing.
And then: the pink lines on the test,
a wish come too late.

    There will be no baby now.
    Appointments made, the clinic
    an hour's drive away, winding and meandering roads.

Your boxes long packed, wedding ring removed
as if it had never sat heavy on your hand.
We do not discuss the particulars of your decision—
words like *addiction*, *despair* too predictable,
unnecessary when we talk about your husband. We both know
who he is.

And now, we look up at the snowy mountains,
spring still seeming so far away.

THIS IS THE LAST TIME

crushed candy

Before that spring, fields were just fields. We'd crossed the empty fields behind the Civic Centre countless times, a shortcut home, a shortcut to the market where we would fill our pockets with chocolate bars, licorice whips, gummy bears. Then, they were just fields.

1985, and we were innocent. Our streets were busy with kids, shouts from mothers calling us in for dinner. We played kick the can. Freeze tag. Red light, green light. Bicycles were strewn on lawns, forgotten. But then, he took the girls in that field. We knew them. They were us.

Whispers passed between mothers, assemblies were held at school, where we were warned not to go anywhere with a stranger, where we were told to always remain in groups. Now, even walking in twos was unsafe. He had changed that. Our mothers turned the TVs on low when newscasts came on, but still we heard enough. We knew he had hurt them, but could not yet imagine how. Yellow Neighbourhood Watch stickers went up in windows. Mothers drove us to school in the morning now. Our fathers added new deadbolts to the doors. A gesture only, we knew, because those girls had been taken in daylight, the hours that were supposed to be safe.

What else did we know? Candy was crushed beneath the girl, sticky and gummy on the back of her T-shirt. The field would have been warming from early spring sun. Moments before, the girls had purchased slushies and five-cent candies at the market across the street. The sting of sugar still on their tongues.

It didn't matter how he got them there—each lie worked, worked just as well as on all those other girls. The list grew, endless, spooling out. Vancouver, Langley, Burnaby. His fingerprints across all that geography. He put a paper bag over his head. He said, Make love to me. What do little girls know about love? The girl shut her eyes. He told her friend to watch.

There were birds in the trees, trilling about spring coming early. The sound of laughter echoed from the street beyond, other kids walking home from school, their backpacks heavy with math worksheets, social studies textbooks. The girls heard them, and prayed for someone to trample the long grass, save them. They didn't even know what being saved would look like. But still, they were so close. The laughter was clear.

When he was done, he put the gun in his waistband, told them to count to one hundred before moving. They counted, obedient still, before staggering to the street. Bloodied, shaking, no longer girls.

The friend picked candy berries from the girl's back, dropped them to the dirt as if they were white-hot.

tracks

I do not dream of the boy who believed he could outwit a train,
his body sliced neatly in half
but no swift death;
for months he lay in a ward in another country,
sleeping a deep, dreamless sleep,
body grieving itself. The impossibility that any part of him survived.
No death from smoke inhalation,
third-degree burns, as we might have imagined for him—
now a long, lingering death, one drunken night in a train yard.

But I do remember when we were younger,
my boyfriend his best friend,
watching them on a football field,
believing them invincible.
Then, when I knew more words for love than I do now.
When mortality was imperceptible, impossible,
and we imagined ourselves one day old, one day ready.

one set of tracks

on hearing Anne Caston read

Despite your pink satin shoes
you speak of carrying a body–
  infant, unformed, translucent–
to the water.
Swathed in pink and cream
(a confectioner's dream)
I watch your hands—ringless, slender—
but cannot imagine them
  lifting
a child from the table,
another from a water pipe,
tying lengths of stained cloth
around bloodless limbs.

Instead, you belong on a covered porch
in the South of your youth,
a bowl of sugar peas in your hands,
the snap—break—and drop into the bowl
the only sound in the evening shade.

But I am left with this:
a boy's running shoes, darkened with dirt,
and yours—shimmering, pale pink—
belying the muddy path
  on which you walked.

Room 502

The rope swinging
smudged handprints on the windowsill
   don't jump just stop cut her down
busy years—
1928 with the young nurse's slender feet—
stockinged only, she had taken time to remove
                    her dark shoes
hanging now only in white—
followed by another nurse crawling onto the windowsill
bracing herself against a clear sky
                                        a tipping over of blue
before propelling herself forward—
        hem of white cotton lifted
   kited with gravity—
and then the shadow on the floor
the tapping at the window frame.

The fifth floor held the mad
(red rubber ball echoing in hallways)
their lungs not immune, still filling
   still expanding, pushing out
and perhaps this is why the air held white
their smocks shifted in breeze
pulling away from blued limbs
that once held the bars of a patient's bed
pushed it to the open porch
   (fresh air: recommended)
and watched the tree line beyond.

Those moments of pure escape from the fifth floor
the lightness of air around their white robes—
all suspended.

Their whiteness

framed by the window (mid-flight)
the other more stationary
only the breeze interrupting
                    (ball ever echoing)
                    voices muffled by gauze
                                    hard hands
                    the sound of lungs cracking
                                    that hiss of air.

Similkameen River, 1921

They went down to the river.

The house quiet when he returned,
water buckets gone,
meaning only: river.
He leaves his school books in their hemp sack,
goes back out into the snowy day.
The closer he gets, the deeper the footprints:
he steps in his mother's
as if he is invisible.

Footprints down to the bank—
  one large, one small, mother, sister—
but none in retreat.

And at the edge of the river, nothing.
Only two upturned water buckets
and the rush of the river,
not yet frozen—greedy to move
while it's still possible.

He would not remember
his sprint to the mine
(X miles without stopping once)
or the exact words uttered to his father,
nor the run back—
          quickly quickly in case
          they might still be—
          we might pull them out—
only his panicked collapse
when he realized he could not see them in the water,
there was no pulling them out.

His father, shortly behind him,

hands black, made blacker still against
the snow, the ice, the river,
finds the boy face down in the snow,
body slack, eyes glazed,
holding him like an empty sack
as he ran back toward their empty house.

No more bodies to find,
to carry with him—
only the abandoned water buckets,
a shoe, rock upturned at river's edge,
small things to tuck away in pockets.

Bridgend County

images from South Wales

> "There is another world, and they who
> kill themselves to accompany their friend
> thither, will live with them there."
> —Druid maxim

There is too much blood on this land.

Hundreds of years ago, monks converted Celts—
  baptisms where their pagan spirits were drowned,
  churches instead built on ancient pagan sites—
in these copses. Below these very trees.

Now, nooses
are left on tree branches as reminders,
jute unravelling in the rain.

All those kids who knew too much about black lung—
their fathers coming home full of dust,
lasting long after the coal mines were closed,
their towns turned bleaker still—
tying knots in ropes and hanging from trees
in these ugly, lovely towns.
Clusters of sorrow.

The Romans came through here,
the Vikings, the Normans.
On All Saints' Day, the Celts dressed up as ghosts
to protect themselves
against the restless spirits of the dead.

Now, a cluster of almost a hundred restless spirits.
This is, after all, Druid heartland.

There are farmlands, empty fields,
little girls chasing one another in gardens,
terraced houses where someone is baking a cake,
stirring honey into tea.
Roads that wind over ridges,
valleys, and valleys.

Still, the girls and boys are found
swinging in morning air,
and the others will cut them down,
the weight of their bodies too much.

elegy for teen girls

The girls are disappearing.
Some slip into rivers, never to return,
others left on embankments,
already forgotten.
Still others take pills, tie ropes around their necks,
reclaiming their bodies as their own.

In a leafy suburb, another girl remained silent,
the way she was taught to do,
until she overdosed, getting it right the second time.

This new world is full of flashes and photos;
everything is permanent.
Even the images of their bodies bent, slack,
passed from boy to boy. There is no way to unsee.

The rivers are no longer simple to navigate—
too many girls have been pulled from uncertain depths,
naked girls, bloated girls, girls in garbage bags like so much trash.
The current always threatening to pull more girls under.
So we pray, instead, that they will remember the breaststroke, the
whip kick,
that their hands will cut sure lines in the swells,
carving a way out, away from the current—
that they are strong enough for this,
that they have been practising for this moment all along.

at Grand Street, I sat down and wept

on Elizabeth Smart

You did not see the flames,
the spines of your books turning to ash,
to nothingness,
as if their thin pages had never existed.
But still you dream of the scratch of the match.

His words would not be burned,
you think as you pin the nappies,
push the pram, mash the peas.
Launder what's soiled.
But yours: the hiss of the match.

Knowing his influence would turn to the stuff of legend—
only one suggestion you took, just the change of title—
and you'd be held aloft as *protégé*,
some other, equally small word for *woman*.

safe as houses

The house in a shaggy field,
long abandoned, unroofed, stippled with moss.
Given back to the elements,

some kind of ancient sacrifice,
shot through with ivy and cattails. Flowers in the doorframe.
Yet still you went in,

stepped over broken bottles and used condoms,
into rooms forgotten: mouldering sofa, rusting metal bedframe,
cracked kitchen table left behind like a foundling,

as if the owners had absquatulated,
fleeing even their own fingerprints on the furniture.
In each room you envisioned how the house would once have been—

everything copacetic, lemon-printed curtains on the windows,
frilling in the spring breeze. Orderly.
Once cared for, the kitchen counters scrubbed clean, glowing.

In the basement, a tiny, lost bedroom,
a bunk and a wardrobe, a box full of letters in tidy cursive,
a mourning sampler, and a daguerreotype of an unsmiling man.

Sorrow begets sorrow.

The basement is shadowy and dank,
the basement of all your childhood fears—
dark corners, cold drafts, subterranean.

These are the wonders, bombastic beliefs
that houses hold secrets,
that they are more than plaster or drywall.

Placing shoes on a table brings bad luck.
A swarm of bees foretells a fire.
An old broom brings along bad luck.

And still you go through the rooms,
run your hands over swollen walls,
believe that the house holds your own dark memories.

You walk backwards out of the house,
careful to touch all the same spots, superstitious, ritualistic,
and close the warped front door behind you.

What does it matter in the end?
Perhaps nothing at all—
it's just wood and nails, paint and cement,

just a place where, once, you hung a jacket,
or slept in a souring, narrow bed,
or lit a match, opened a door, walked away.

unveiled

on St. Clare's Monastery, Mission, B.C.

I

You notice the coifs first, tucked neatly under the nuns' veils,
when they come out in the early morning into the garden
with its roric grass, pale sunlight, between prayers.
The nuns are cloistered, praying seven times a day,
the sound of their hymns clear, crystalline,
their voices full as they sing for Jesus.

II

They cut back roses with their capable hands, trim the hydrangea,
exposing pith to the new spring air from their perch on the mountaintop,
the Fraser River a frisson of rushing water below.

You watch for the rust-brown robes on the grounds of the monastery,
watch for the nuns—silent, their lives dedicated to prayer and poverty—
as they work side by side in the dappled sunlight.

You've never been inside the monastery,
but imagine it cavernous, commodious,
altars and candles and soft-paged Bibles.
You do not know what must transpire to bring the women here,
if they had once been desperate, feckless,
or if they felt called, tethered to Jesus,
to a god who judged them only by the content of their souls.

III

And still you can't help but imagine each nun in her closed, quiet
  room,
puddling a brown habit on the ground
before stepping into a full tub to wash away the last traces of dark
  soil,
body bare in the warm water,
her breasts and thighs, soft stomach exposed,
made ordinary once again.

Operation Persistence

> "diving through the shuddering
> wet world, carries us"
> Eleonore Schönmaier

Things wash up on the shore for weeks after the crash—
a pair of velour trackpants,
a small blanket with a rough, woollen weave,
a cluster of plastic baby toys—
lion, giraffe, alligator—
and because you had taken the boat out that day,
when the Search and Rescue still hoped to find any survivors,
you pocket the alligator, because somebody should remember.
You run your fingers over its bumpy head, jaw,
and try to remember if alligators have gnathic bones,
but that makes you think about how the passengers
could not be identified,
how even bones do not mean witness.

Usually, you use the boat to fish for pickerel,
later dusting it with flour and lemon,
when you would gorge
on the fish standing over the kitchen sink,
every so often pulling a stray bone from your teeth.
Those days, you were gentle with the boat, unhurried,
letting it scissor the waves around Peggy's Cove.

But not that day.

The crash into the Atlantic Ocean ensorcelled you—
you believed they could be saved, that they were there,
just below the water's lip,
and you'd pull them carefully onto the boat,
cover them with blankets that still smelled of winter,
of ice and sharp cold, the memory of a pair of mittens, a toboggan,

deep within the fabric.
But that day was late summer, maybe edging into fall,
and you did not collect anyone in your boat,
just kept spinning in useless serpentine circles in the bay,
looking for even one hand in the shuddering, wet world,
                        waving.

January, the coldest month

on my grandfather's death

The morning you died, ice and snow blanketed the field beyond.
The rain had not started yet,
and still birds trilled on branches made heavy by snow,
believing in spring.

Inside, paramedics and police officers and funeral home
representatives
lined up, dressed tidily in black
offering condolences that sounded like rain in metal bowls—
the ping, the sting.

They would take you away,
shoes careful on the ice and snow,
leaving the apartment airless with your absence.

The clocks ticked out of sync,
the little hand in endless chase.

Everywhere, reminders of your life unspooling:
photos tacked and stacked against one another,
porcelain figurines of flowers, and one an old woman with her dog,
bowls of candies, butterscotch and hard chocolate,
handwritten notes on the fridge, reminding you of doctors' phone
numbers,
birthdays, inspirational quotes,
all the necessary detritus of life.
The rooms suddenly too hot, stale.

Outside, the trees bowed, graceful and laced with ice,
and tiny birds skipped from limb to limb.
They knew nothing of your death.
The cold felt right, necessary,
as if to harden the grief unfurling.

If we breathed in deeply enough,
surely we would feel ice in the lungs.

After they took you away,
the rooms were closed up, locked tight with finality.
We could no longer look at your softened leather couch,
the rumpled bedsheets, your rocking chair.
When we stepped into the new afternoon, it began to rain.
As it should.

capacity for love

I sprinkled your ashes in the garden,
under the rose you planted for me.
It bloomed and bloomed all summer,
the peach-pink-orange blossoms bowing the limbs,
the entire backyard infused with that heady scent.
You were in the garden with us then,
teaching me how to cut the roses back,
telling me (again) the story of bringing the rose all the way from
   Germany,
a gift for my grandmother,
your abundant love all there in full bloom.

floating practice

All the children float face down in the pool,
pretending to have drowned.
Behind them, the mass of ancient trees,
the high sun,
a benign afternoon set adrift by all their bodies
littering the pool's surface.

You think of the summer you were four,
when a neighbour fell into your family pool—
unable to swim, her water wings abandoned on the pool deck.
How quickly your father ran across the yard,
how crisp his shallow dive into that chlorinated blue,
coming up with the girl coughing water in his arms.

Then, everyone had clapped, relieved,
as if it were nothing more than performance,
something other than a few seconds from tragedy.

Then, you hadn't considered how your father must have felt,
coming out of the pool with a child in his arms,
the weight of her small body.
How he must have shaken once he deposited her,
still coughing, on her mother's lap,
as the adrenalin left his system.
How the water must have pooled under his feet,
reminding him of what had just happened,
had almost happened,
how the weight of her, pulling her up up up,
would have felt so much like pulling you up from the water.

Now, you smear suntan lotion on your daughter,
trying to delay her jump into the pool
until all the children turn over, gulp air,
are made alive once again.

She dives in,
slicing the water with her sure strokes,
coming up for air again,
              and again.

the girls in the back row compare engagement rings

They wave diamonds at one another, holding their hands high,
gush over size and sparkle and shine.

Over half the girls in the winter term will get engaged,
spend the last weeks of classes planning wedding parties,

distracted by the exact shade of lilac for bridesmaid dresses.
In the summer, they'll marry in white dresses with high hopes,

in backyards and clapboard churches,
receptions with no wine, no beer,

just water jugs and lilies in mason jars.
In the fall, they come back pregnant,

their bellies growing bigger as the weeks carry on,
each worrying over how many onesies they have,

how much a crib costs,
if they can borrow someone's stroller.

Half again will not finish their degrees,
the other half will plan to become teachers or nurses,

spending endless hours caring, soothing, worrying,
their hands turning dry, red, chapped, angry.

The girls will bring their babies back to campus,
passing them around to the other girls, who coo and fuss.

They hand in papers about the beauty of maternity,
the dark underside of feminism.

They refuse to read articles on gender or religion.
They do not want to read poems about sex.

Every fall, we learn new names for these girls,
their own last names wiped clean

with the changing of the seasons,
as if they never existed at all.

beyond the summer garden

She brings me handfuls of black feathers,
proud of her discovery, their softness, the arcing quills.
She does not understand when I brush them from her palms,
wash her hands twice in the deep sink.

This summer, there were bones in her playhouse,
small, white, picked clean,
as if an uninvited guest had dined,
cooking on her tiny plastic stove.
Later, we found wasps; nests in the eaves.

Now, the feathers. Dark omens.
She does not understand what it is to hold death,
how these animals come to be, and then are not.
The weight of bones.

Later we swim, her tiny arms sure in the water,
her skin golden from the sun.
We bury the bones. Knock away the wasps' nests. Collect and hide
  the feathers.
Then, watch her even strokes under the water,
the way she always comes up, face held high to the sun.
The way she plunges under again,
sure of my hands to pull her up,
and up and up and up,
holding her aloft in the summer air.

playing dead

There is something vaguely white, vaguely grey,
just below the lip of the swimming pool's water—
turned green over the winter,
scattered now with leaves and pine needles—
and you immediately think, a possum.
  The horror of having to scoop the bloated body
  out of the water,
  the weight of it in the net, threatening to rip.

Once, there was a possum in your parents' pool,
floating on its back, dumb eyes wide, long tail spooling out.
Your father must have taken it out, buried it somewhere,
but you never saw.
Then, there were always possums crossing your backyard
because of the mink farm down the road,
that deep, oily, animal smell
unbearable on warm nights when the air was still and thick.
You remember seeing their shining eyes
in the darkened backyard
lit only by the spill of moonlight.

You doubt you are strong enough to lift the possum from the water,
to hold a dead body in your hands.
                    You think this is the only time you miss having a
                      husband,
                    delegating death to him.

The water shimmers, breaks when you tentatively put the net in.
Push past the leaves, the pine needles,
peer into the dark green depths.
The vaguely white, vaguely grey thing moves,
shifts with the water's disturbance.
You close your eyes, waiting for the moment of contact,
when net meets death and transfers that energy

up the pole to your hands.
You push deeper, scoop up as if this is muscle memory.

The net is full of decaying hydrangea blooms,
huge, filigreed white mopheads
that look nothing like a possum.
Relief. Laughter. Death has not touched you today,
but you have buried something anyway.

sharp things

The summer he left, sharp things were everywhere: pointed quills of lost feathers, wasps, disappointment. You collected them in your hands, everything dark and maybe dangerous.

It was strange, how the wasps just gave up, stunning themselves on the windows. You watched their wings flutter, stuttering against the glass. But you couldn't bring yourself to kill them—you understood their last, desperate attempts at life.

You gathered the bodies. You walked the lawn, collecting dark, oily feathers. You believed that, at any moment, he would appear at the back gate, apologetic and shamed.

The wasps buzzed. The feathers fell. The seasons turned, and still the gate did not squeak. And finally, your hands turned red, pricked too many times.

lemonade

You pull lemon rinds from the sink,
after you remember that you cannot put them in the garburator,
your hands still blameless
before they touch the yellow skins.
You have an irrational fear
of putting your hand in the garburator, its blades spontaneously
   spinning,
shredding the skin of your fingers.
You blame this on old horror movies,
though you do not know if this is true.
So many potential wounds terrify you:
      your Achilles tendon rupturing, rolling like a ribbon;
      childbirth; laser eye surgery, the laser missing,
      burning through your eye.
      So many failures, so many ways to hurt.

You used the lemons to make a pitcher of lemonade
wanting the sharp spike of it in your throat,
but you added too much sugar and everything was too sweet,
the wrong texture, the wrong mixture on your tongue.
You wanted acid, some kind of pain,
as if to prove you could feel something still.
You imagined dropping the pitcher,
letting the glass explode on the hardwood floor,
maybe stepping on a shard.
Bright blood. Clean slice.
It's not the pain you want,
but something other than this numb chill.

Instead, you put the pitcher in the fridge,
as if you might drink it later,
imagining your mangled fingers,
a strange penance
for something you don't quite understand.

night visitors

I expected my grandfather, at least,
to visit me after he died:
a vision, a feeling, a chill just above my breastbone.
I waited for it, but it never came—
he remained silent, gone,
an absence only.

My grandmothers died before him,
soundlessly and swiftly,
and it pained me that I saw any affinity to them
only after it was too late—
I understood their unhappiness,
the exact shape and size of their disappointment and rage.
A strange inheritance passed down,
the weight of it suffocating.

Happiness seemed too foreign,
too abstract,
and I learned to expect so much less.

One grandmother did not speak to my grandfather
for two long years.
They moved past each other in their small white house,
the only sound the birds cawing outside.
The other dutifully waited on her husband,
every day longer than the last,
the tinkle of his teacup against saucer
a call for her.

Shapes of sorrow, specific and sharp.

I heard their whispers in strange moments,
their voices an echo of worry or affirmation.

I could only recognize them in myself years later,
more bruised, more broken.

How did we survive on so little?

My grandfather still has not visited me,
but my grandmothers continue to whisper,
Be cautious, be careful with your heart, be cruel if you must.

mirrors

My daughter steals my clothes, my shoes, my pyjamas,
and this is new territory for us—
she was a baby only a moment ago.
Already, she looks so much older than she has ever been,
her face all new angles,
sharp cheekbones, pinked lips.
She pulls on my hoodie
and when her face emerges, I'm left breathless,
because her face is my face,
her expressions the ones that I casually wear.

Cashiers in grocery stores tell us how much we look alike,
and my daughter rolls her eyes, perpetually annoyed,
but I revel in the fact that we mirror each other,
that my genes punched up through her,
that we share these visceral things:
our faces, our expressions, the way we toss our hair.

Some nights, she watches movies in my bed with me—
she wants horror, loves to see me jump,
loves to see fear flash across my face.
She falls asleep with her head against my shoulder,
snoring and sweet.
Her face the same as when she was born,
startling still.

One day, she'll wear my rings, my necklaces,
will sleep in my bedroom alone,
or maybe with someone else,
unhappiness a foreign concept,
still wearing my expressions, perhaps more of my clothes,
and maybe—maybe—she will be thankful then
to look like me,
surprised when she sees my smile on her face
 when she looks in the mirror.

this is the last time

after a poem by Tishani Doshi

Girls are coming out of the woods,
noctambulant and beatific,
heads bent, hands held under the moonlight,
each spine straight and sure
of their destination, their destiny.
Around them, the trees watch silently,
stoic in their solemn witness.
Girls are coming out of the woods.
Raccoons and mice hurry out of their way,
girls once broken, beaten, forgotten
at the bottom of a bog,
in a shallow lake,
under the wax seal of a mountain grave.
Now they cross the forest,
their faces aglow, peachy again,
as they had been so many months and years before.
Girls are coming out of the woods,
lighting candles, letting the wax spill to the earth below,
leaving a viscous trail,
forever a line of girls shrouded by candlelit vigils,
a grave funerary toast,
remembering mnemonics for grief,
their faces plastered on roadside broadsides and milk cartons.
They are coming out of the woods, into new sunlight.
They run.

RECKLESS

scatter

for Serina

If you hold the photo at a certain angle,
it could be us today:
still blonde, still thin, still with heads tilted toward each other,
almost the versions we remember from twenty years ago.

Nineteen, and we'd already experienced death—
the boy catapulted through a car window,
another putting a gun in his mouth, not hesitating before he pulled
the trigger—
we'd already had sex with boys we shouldn't have
we'd imagined we knew the world around us in some unique way.

Then, we didn't yet know how life could tilt,
the disappointment of husbands,
the exquisite, terrifying love for our children.
We were thinking about the boy in the field,
ejected from the car at 2 a.m.,
his body briefly suspended in macabre flight.

It would be another year before a girl from high school
died in a parked car at Hunter Park,
her boyfriend in the driver's seat,
the car still running, but their bodies too still.
We thought, *That could be us.*
And for a while, we were careful, cautious—
we insisted on condoms, drank tap water in bars—
until we believed again in our immortality.

You'd move to a mountaintop,
and I'd stay on the coast. Salt and snow between us.
We made the three-hour journey on the TransCanada Highway,
windows rolled down, wind rushing in to ruffle our hair,
intermingling strands of ash and gold.

Now, we watch our children play on the grass
beneath a deeply pink summer sunset.
They shriek and laugh, scatter
like so many seeds across the yard.
Do we think of those other lost boys and girls,
other bodies landing, broken, on dew-soaked grass?

We call to the children, gather them up,
wrap them in blankets, perhaps too tightly, our fingers lingering,
stunned by our own impossible luck.

wasps

The wasps are committing suicide in the pool
when the last man you slept with calls to tell you everything
he wants to do to your body.
He talks about your breasts, and you want to concentrate
but you can't stop watching the drowning black-and-yellow bodies,
the way their wings shudder with water weight
as they try to stay above the surface.
You could scoop them out with the net,
could deposit them gently on the grass,
but you do not. You count them,
dismayed that so many could be there at once,
lured in by the chlorine, the salt.
You want the man to be doing all the things he describes,
not just saying them. You want less distance between you,
you want no distance at all,
instead his body pressed against you in the swimming pool,
his hands and mouth busy on you while, around you both,
all these tiny bodies are dying.

burn

You're writing poems on blank postcards, the backs of receipts,
because they are easier to tear up and burn
in the copper pot.
(The one you bought for New Year's when you wrote down the things
you wanted to end, and burned them
in the deep porcelain sink, the flames satisfying in their lick.)

Do you have the words to write what you really need to say?
Each one tastes bitter, not weighty enough
when you hold it in your mouth.

You want to write about the way paper dissolves when it's in water
too long.
The way leather smells when lit on fire.
The way gold doesn't burn or dissolve or disappear,
the way it remains even when you don't want it to:
infinity, the symbol on your finger.

You write about black feathers on the lawn,
a man in your bed,
the woman you don't want to think about
(the painful reminder that you had put your feet in stirrups,
asked the doctor for every test,
the shame, there, blanched).
It's so easy to rip up,
to erase, to burn.

At night, your daughter crawls into your bed,
reaches out for you.
She presses her small body against you,
all heat and sweat and need,
and you think those are the words you should write—
the way she talks in her sleep,
the creases on her forehead when she dreams,

and her hands forever seeking you out,
wanting the surety of your body there beside her,
your heartbeat strong and steady, still.

turns to will

What's the old saying? It's like ripping the bandage off?
Now: your heart, the bandage;
the rip, his body.
It's been almost twenty years since another man
has seen you naked,
and you expect to be bashful, cautious,
but instead your body is greedy
for this heat, this need
so close to the surface.
It's bursting made physical.

You don't care about the C-section scar
(and secretly you love it a little),
that shimmering pink line slightly raised like earthworms,
or the weight of your breasts in his hands.

This is pleasure: the precise feeling of only feeling—
no thought behind the way you reach for him,
the first time in so many years
that you have been just body.
Just want. *Want* such an underrated word.
Want turns to will turns to was. Turns to.
In the morning, you move together wordlessly—
you can feel him memorizing every part of your body
because you both know this will not happen again.
You can't rip a bandage off twice.

nineteen

When you ask me if I remember
the night we drove out to the beach
and I returned with sand in my hair,
rinsing myself clean in your shower after,
I know what you are really asking:
Do I remember all the times we fucked,
all the times you held your hands against my ribs,
your lips at my throat? I do:
all those years of fast cars and smoky rooms.
And so the past collides with the present
and we're both nineteen again,
wanting mouths and lips and hands,
both of us smelling like the ocean, salt left sticky on our skin.
How many times? you ask, and I cannot answer.
One hundred? Two hundred? Maybe more.
We are excavating the past—slowly, purposefully,
maybe painfully,
maybe because we both know something is just out of reach,
we are almost there, me in a green lace bra,
you rolling on a condom—
but somehow we pulled away from each other
until there were too many cities, too many hours between us.
But still: those salt-filled nights,
the wind coming in through the open windows,
the car gliding over the centre line, and the ocean so close
we could feel it on our bare skin
like your tongue—later, on my navel,
both of us arching up
for something we couldn't yet name.
The past keeps arriving because we hold it in our mouths,
will it into being—
if we say it, it jumps alive in our minds:
your hands, your mouth, my body on the car's bench seat—
and maybe we never really left that time,

maybe we are still there, almost at the beach,
almost loving each other.

ruins

Your mother told you it would ruin you
if you let a boy do *that*,
as she rolled out the pastry for butter tarts,
her back to you in the kitchen, raisins scattered,
sugar dusting the countertop.
Even at sixteen, you knew what she meant by *that*,
by the way her mouth puckered as she said the words,
tasting something too sour.
                    You knew she meant letting a boy fuck you
because you had already let a boy fuck you—
on a waterbed, in the back seat of a yellow station wagon,
once on a couch at a party while "Heart-Shaped Box" played in the
    next room.
The bite of leather on your bare skin,
hot breath, the boy's hipbones jabbing
into the soft flesh of your thighs.
                    Later, purpling-black bruises laced your thighs,
and when you touched them you heard *Hey! Wait! Hey! Wait!*

Your mother did not say what kind of ruin,
                    and so instead you thought of St. Rule's Tower in St.
                        Andrews,
                    where a boy jumped from the top, angled his body
                    to the rocky shore of the North Sea below.
                    The tower ancient, crumbling,
                    the brackish ocean air eating through the sandstone,
                    leaving behind only the lick of salt,
                    the only memory that there once had been so much
                        more.

You knew she didn't mean that kind of ruin,
though your body was also salt-stained after you fucked that boy.

And so you never tell her about the other boys,
or the way a body can open in so many ways,
can sharpen to bone, can cleave.
The many ways a body can wound,
            the ways the body is a wound.

Years later, when a man warns you that he will ruin you,
you think, *Yes*,
            or maybe, *Already broken*,
and you'll be at the top of that ancient tower,
the sea so blue and tempting below you,
                                    just asking you to jump.

breadcrumbs

You let him do whatever he wants to your body. Somehow, you trust him—trust him more than your ex-husband, trust him in ways that dismay you. He is sometimes gentle, sometimes not, but the bruises on your body are welcome, are just markers of mouths on bodies, hands on bodies, and there is something beautiful in the purple blooms. Your thighs. Your breasts. You let him do whatever he wants to your body. He kisses you on the sidewalk in front of the bar where you've had too much tequila. Kisses you on the sidewalk again. Again. Again. Again. Kisses you on the train, where a teenage girl watches you both, her mouth open in wonder or want. Later, in the dim light of the apartment, you let him peel your clothes off, and they litter the floor like so much detritus. Your clothes from a fairy tale, a line of bread crumbs from kitchen to hallway to bedroom. Maybe you could find your way in the dark. Maybe you could find your way back to him in the dark. You feel his lips on you, his hands on you, and you think, *This*. You let him do whatever he wants to your body. This is not difficult, not an offering of any kind. You let him do what he wants because this is the only reasonable thing for you to do.

reckless

Both of my grandmothers were wildly unhappy—one meant to visit the better-loved first wife's grave every summer holiday, and the other meant to move from Dundee to Merritt, where the sidewalks were wooden and she stepped in horse shit. They stayed with their husbands, let their rage simmer, sparking just below the surface. They are long gone when I tell my husband to leave, and still I hear their *tsk tsk* in my ears, hear their whispered, *You can survive this, you are strong enough to stay.* I let the months pass, and still they whisper at me. *Don't break things. Don't be selfish. You can make do with less.* And then, when I let a man in my bed, when I let him fuck me however he wants, I hear them say, *Reckless, reckless,* and when I let him do it again and again, I hear them repeat, *Reckless, reckless,* but it's softer, an afterthought, and I now hear the quiet want behind it, confirmation that, yes, this is what I am meant to do.

this is not a love poem

You lay in my crumpled bed, reading poems
I had written for someone else.
Only hours before, you had been inside me,
but somehow this is more intimate,
the vulnerability of choice of words, the way I use *almost*
when I mean *very much*,
the way that language is a cage, protecting those parts of myself
too tender to expose to air.

cherry popsicles

I had almost forgotten about that time in drama class when I had
to be the girl in the play—
you know, the one in every play, *the girl*—
and I had to lie perfectly still in the centre of the stage with my
eyes closed
while everyone else took turns putting a hand on me,
recreating the trauma in the play through touch,

on shoulder or knee or elbow or.
I had consented to this,
had been asked in a quiet room by my drama teacher because,
she said,
You're strong enough for this.
It never occurred to me to say no, to say that I didn't think I was
strong at all.

And now I think of all the other hands that have
touched me,
breast or stomach or ass or.
Some because I wanted them to, some not.
And I wonder if each of those handprints remain,
just below the surface of my skin,
a topographical map of how touch shapes us,
redefines us.

After that drama class, I was excused from math and biology,
sat backstage with another girl and ate cherry flavoured
popsicles.
My drama teacher said I'd done well, as she knew I would,
but all I could think about was the way those hands felt smeared
across my skin,
the way the light behind my eyes dazzled and disappeared,
the ways I would have to be strong, later.

the haunting

a cento, taken from poems by Hala Alyan, Kayla Czaga, and Maggie Smith

Everything haunts: sex, hands,
fortune tellers, swans, love boats.
We needed a word for everything before—
every wound reveals its own repair.
I am standing in a cemetery,
because a lie is not a lie if the teller believes it.

sours

You pickle the eggplant in an old mason jar—
garlic, white vinegar, parsley, red pepper flakes, salt—
crack the carapace of the prawns, slicing cleanly through muscle.

These are things your hands know how to do—
cut, create, feed the ones you love.

You toss the scraps in the bin, open a bottle of your great-aunt's wine,
so strong it stings the back of your throat.
Before she died, she said she had learned the process while bootlegging,
making whisky and gin and wine in small batches
(farmhouse sink, bathtub)
but no one really believed her.
By then she was older than you'd ever imagined possible,
all lethargy and loneliness and lies,
reading a romance paperback with a creased, cracked cover while she drank her wine.
She'd had so many husbands, so many lovers, you couldn't keep track.
She did not understand your want for one man, for possession.

Everything bubbles and gurgles on the stove,
as you wait for him to arrive. Impatient, your heart skittering in your chest.
His mouth on your neck, your pulse. His hands greedy, always.
He once took you to a rooftop to see a dovecote.
The cooing was louder than the wind in that peristeronic palace,
and you touched a dove's breath-soft feathers
as he pressed up against you from behind, the heat from him nearly scalding you.
Desire in so many forms.

Your great-aunt claimed she lived with the man
who accidentally
came up with the word *octothorpe* in the late '60s—
a cottage with a blue door, she said, and the softest bed she'd ever slept in.
She said the word alone made her remember every orgasm she'd had with him
octothorpe, octothorpe, octothorpe
and the one time she'd pointed a carving knife at his heart.
Love, she said, and shrugged, *is complicated*.

And now, with your hand on a knife, you wonder what he might be remembered for—
the words he's written for you? A dark mood, a hard heart?
Loving you, even a little?

You stir the sauce, you let the prawns cool,
you drink the wine that prickles your throat, welcoming its bitter bite,
the way it sours when you hold it in your mouth for too long,
and you watch the door, willing it to open.

manmade

They made the lake when they created the subdivision of expensive, expansive houses, a lake filled with non-native fish, and unnatural shores of trucked-in sand. Nothing about it was natural. Nothing about it was true.

You go down to the lake one night with your best friend, her older brother, and his friends. It feels taut, dangerous to be under the moonlight with them—boys three years older than you, boys who can drive, boys with the beginnings of moustaches—and their bodies so close to yours. They laugh, they pop open beer cans, they look at you for a moment too long.

One of them decides to take the canoe out, and your best friend agrees to go with him. The lake is not wide, is not long; you'll be able to see the canoe the whole time. But still, you feel a flutter in your stomach when she gets into it, when the boy pushes off, silently, from the lakeshore. You watch until you can no longer really see her, until her head seems to slip below the demarcation of the canoe's edge.

Your best friend's brother gives you a beer, and you drink it without wanting it. He puts his clammy hand on the back of your neck, a gesture you hate, and you take a small step away. The sand gives way under your step. It's shifting, uncertain.

You watch the canoe glide further across the lake. The lake has never seemed so big, so unending. You wonder if your best friend will ever come back.

The other boy hands you a cigarette, but you don't want it either. You look up at the dark night sky, the way the stars hang untethered, and you listen as the boys talk. Their voices low, lower, their laughter a slap. One reaches out to touch your arm. The other watches. You feel the weight of them both, the way you must placate them and encourage them all at once. Tilt your head. Nod. Laugh, even when you don't want to.

Your best friend's brother decides this is lame, he's over it. You watch him go up the hill to his house, all shadow, inky in the black night. The other boy stays. This boy has put his arms around you once. Has touched the back of your neck in a different way. This boy has been good and decent, all the other things you are taught you should look for in boys. This boy smiles at you. Looks at you like you are a feast—every inch of you a pleasure, a hot spot, a point.

He puts his hand out, touches your waist.

The canoe is still gone. The lake is calm. There is no one coming back. No returning.

This other boy lights another cigarette, and you watch the amber burn of it. The way it glows, almost beautiful, in the dark.

And then he's holding it out to you, the lit end too close to your breasts, just there, and it ignites—the flame catches a stray strand of your long hair, and it lights up, travelling up your sweater, along your chest, and you do not move, cannot even think until—*somehow*—the flame burns out, burns out, runs out of oxygen, and you are left feeling the heat, feeling the sharp spark of ignition.

shards, or the things I will never tell you

your eyes on me like I'm a miracle/your hands on my face/
                the sound of your voice when you said come
your mouth on my neck/
you pressed close to me in the kitchen/you, naked on the patio in
   the night air/
                      your hands in my hair/
                                 //the heat of you

I think *first husband* and it feels so hopeful it breaks me
                I want you to be turning the music on, loud, in my
                   house
I marked the page in a poetry book with a piece of satin/
                I hold your name in my mouth like a whisper

I want to use the word *reckless* as a placeholder/
                but I know really it means you in my bed

there are so many things to be reckless with   my body my words
   my fragments my heart

my name is all vowels, yours is sharper/   prickled in my
   mouth
I run it over my tongue again and again, wanting to turn the edges
   soft

precognition

When I talk of taking a trip, I mean forever
—Adrienne Rich

You sped on the highway, hurtling us toward the Okanagan:
cabin, lake, slow river in the back.
All that promise, the sharpness of the August heat,
the days unspooling and buttery. Pinprick of joy, fleeting.

///

Mustard greens choked the edge of the river,
and you built an embankment to keep the silvery water at bay,
fill the lacuna that had so recently been there,
carrying wood and stones tenderly in your arms.

You chopped more wood, the axe so sharp and sure in your hands—
I wanted to wrest it from your palm,
let you touch me with that same force instead.

I watched you from the dock, where boats whizzed by,
whirring and wheezing against the water,
the sky above a runny blue, somewhere between cerulean and slate,
birds arcing north, nosing forward, within the clouds.

When you came down to the dock, you were glossed with sweat,
the sheen of it across your back when I put my hand there.

///

How long have we been here?
Long enough to move rocks, chop wood,
to have sex in the cabin, on the beds, and on the '70s kitchen linoleum,
the raised imprint of it on my spine later,
a tattoo of the fury of your hips against mine.

I bake wild blackberry pie, and we eat it with our bare hands,
turning bloody and brazen as animals.
How did we turn this domestic—
  axe and apron, sweat and sun glow—
when we meant to be anything but?

It won't last—does it ever?—but the embankment held,
the river did not migrate,
and you woke me up to inky darkness,
your mouth travelling the terrain of my shoulders, my back,
your lips coming away tasting like sunscreen and sunshine.
Now, your hands wresting something from me—maybe love—
and my heart is a staircase,
a clamour of feet, a balter.

confession

When your best friend tells you that you let men happen to you,
you think, *Yes*. This is exactly what your past is littered with:
men who arrive, decide on you, and your unhappiness unspools.
Where did this impulse come from?
Generations of unhappy women only concerned with survival—
the luxury of happiness too much.
Instead, cigarettes in the afternoon, a pound cake, a coconut
 cream pie,
a tumbler of whisky in the kitchen when no one is looking.
Happiness reflected back like a broken mirror. Shards.

The only men you've chosen have been the ones you actually loved,
the ones who did not last long enough.
Hot breath on your neck, handprints on your body.

Once, you let a wedding happen to you, a whole marriage.
Once, you let a man you did not like in your bed for years.
Once.

How is it possible for love to take such strange forms?
You do not know how to reconcile the past with this unpredictable
 present.
You never did.

//

Your mother is losing her memory, and with it all the things
she disapproves of.

When you were younger,
she told you never to kiss a boy like this or this or this,
she told you never to touch a boy with your warm hands,
never to feel more than he might.
She will not remember that now—

her memory fractured and fractal,
the pieces shifting and rearranging in a random pattern
that you will never understand.

She texts you to ask which country she is in,
where your daughter is tonight,
where her other blue pants are,
and to each question you reply slowly and patiently,
as if that is the person you are.

She calls you one night when you are in bed with a man she's never met,
and while you want to decline the call, you know you cannot.
Her voice is shaky in your ear, and you think she sounds so much older than she is.
You listen to her questions—each one disconnected from the next, from the first,
each one more strange, more unsettling—
as this man's mouth moves across your breasts, your ribs,
each second moving lower and lower.

How do you reconcile her voice on the phone—the confusion, the uncertainty—
and the way he moves deliberately across your body?
You don't.

//

You say to your friend, *My mother has never liked anyone I've been with*,
and as soon as you speak the words, you know they are pure and true.
She will not like this one, as she has not liked any of the men before—
this is the way you communicate:
she disapproves, you withhold. Repeat.

You understand silence, the way it holds weight.
You use it too much—even with this man, even with the others.
Silence feels encased in amber,
something to hold close to your chest.
You say, *I only say no to the men I love,*
knowing your mother will not remember.
You tell her all the things you wanted, the things you liked,
the things you were ashamed of,
a mess of confessions you never imagined you'd utter,
and then there is silence, breath only,
and your mother's voice on the other end of the line,
asking you for the hundredth time,
What did you do today?

wildfires

also for Serina

You are sixteen and ready to shed everything about yourself,
and your best friend has the same itch, the same need,
and so you both race to lose your virginity,
wanting to cast it off, as if it is holding you back.
You fuck your boyfriend (who you actually do not like)
on a waterbed, and you are left with black bruises crawling up your thighs.
She loses hers to a red-headed boy who is not terribly nice, not terribly kind,
and she calls you after, crying about her lost socks.

It was not about the socks.

//

You are twenty-two and standing atop a mountain while you watch your best friend
marry someone she does not love.
Before the ceremony, she cries, and you think, *Yes.*
You hold her in your arms, and then watch her say *I do* twenty-seven minutes later
as the snow falls, and your boots have no traction, and you fear
slipping on the walk to the ski lift.
A groomsman buys you drinks all night,
and you turn hazy, fuzzy as the night goes on.
He says he will walk you back to your room, and you want to say, *Yes YES,*
knowing what *yes* will mean,
but something in you makes you tell him it's okay, you'll be fine.

You are always fine.

//

The province is burning. There are wildfires all through the Interior,
brightly hot, glowing red-orange.
You watch a video of lightning turning a whole town on fire,
and your phone rings at 11:37 p.m., your best friend's voice on the other end.
You've never heard her so panicked, so scared.
She says, *We have to evacuate, we're coming to you,*
and all you can think about is everything they will have to leave behind,
the beds and their hand-knit blankets,
the plants hanging in the den, her paintings on the walls,
the chickens in their coop.
The sky is on fire,
they are packing what they cannot bear to leave behind,
what they can't part with.
You wait.

//

Years later, you sleep with the groomsman
(it feels like more than that, tender and purposeful)
and she leaves her first husband.
More years later, you'll share that too—leaving first husbands
who made you cry, made you feel broken, and so, so small.
But that night, the groomsman looks at you across a bonfire,
and you know exactly what will happen.

//

She sleeps in your spare bedroom,
and you listen to her soft steps in the morning,
as familiar as your own.
You cook eggs, she cuts fruit, you pass books back and forth, wordlessly.

There are so many years between you, so many secrets that you will
never tell—
instead you sit together beside the lake, remembering
all your mistakes, your sorrows, the terrible choices you had to
make,
all the ways you are not the women you meant to be.

tachycardia

He takes a photo of you in his bed—
back bare, your hair falling softly down, loosened and tousled
from the night before—
and the intimacy of the view,
your constellations of freckles so vulnerable,
makes you catch your breath.

The sheets below you a statement,
a possession,
the early-morning sunlight a tell.

//

Last week, you held the fleshy pit of a red plum in your hand,
and for a moment it looked like a bloody heart,
stilled and waiting to pulse.
The heart as muscle, the heart as meat.
The fruit's flesh stained your palm.
A smear of a reminder: hearts break, bleed.

//

Later, he traced the bruises he'd left on your thighs, your ass,
and asked, incredulously, *Did I do this?*
They bloomed dark blue, past indigo, almost black,
and his face flashed with sorrow, remorse,
as if he had intentionally hurt you.
I bruise easily, you said quickly,
putting your hand up to his chest, where you felt his heart beat,
thumping too fast, too hard beneath the thin veneer of his skin.
It's fine, I promise, you said before you put your mouth to his,
still greedy for more.

You pressed on those same bruises later,
as they mottled through purple, green, yellow,
pushed on them until pain spiked through your fingertips.
And you wanted the ache, the throb
so like a heartbeat,
a reminder of how your body became marked this way.
The inconvenience of hearts
and their strange, inconsolable patterns.

You pressed harder.

fractal

Regret is an equation—
you borrow here, subtract there—
all the fractions getting smaller and smaller
until you almost don't remember what it was like
to be whole.

Whole seems impossible now.

In your mind, you keep neat columns
of your regrets:
what you wish you'd done,
what you wish you'd not done.
The second column so much shorter than the first,
it embarrasses you.
You know you are too cautious with love,
unwilling to unfurl,
but this seems like self-preservation,
the heart a tender and bloody muscle.
A half. A fraction.

In one column:
    the words that would not come out of your mouth,
    no matter how purely you meant them,
    banging at your teeth.
    The night he kissed you on the sidewalk
    and you didn't say, *Again. More.*

The other column more simple, less precise:
    married your ex
    stayed with your ex
    lied ever to your daughter.

Whole seems impossible now.

The next man you are with tells you he might love you
on the first night you meet.
You don't mean to, but you say,
You don't even know me,
before he slides into you again.
You aren't sure which kind of regret this will be,
but you are sure it will be one.

When you sleep, his arms firmly around you,
you feel momentarily stitched back together—
not complete, not whole, but something a little less jagged—
and you imagine adding this to one of the columns,
the intricacies of regret so coiled and contained.
You let him sleep, the weight of him against you a quiet relief,
and you stay awake in the dark, like always,
envisioning yourself getting smaller and smaller—
just a hum, just a sigh,
fractured, fractal.

unexpected

The first night you meet,
he tells you that he's going to love you,
and you say, *You don't even know me*,
as he peels your skirt off.
It was only supposed to be one night,
and then you find yourself, months later,
still letting him into your bed,
letting him cook you dinner,
change your car's headlight—
all those little domestic things that you don't want to get used to
because you do not trust affection,
you do not trust love.

> Before, you might have let him love you
> like he wants to—before,
> you might have allowed yourself this joy.
> You think he is too late, he missed the time
> when you were nicer, softer, better.
> You know exactly when you stopped being able to love so easily—
> that other man fucking someone else while your daughter was in the next room.
> You know this, but you still find yourself unable to tell him exactly what you feel:
> something messy and complicated,
> something that flutters in your chest, wings moving too quickly.

When he falls asleep,
his arms are around you
as if he needs to protect you even in sleep,
and you choose to believe that, somehow, you will be able
to let him do whatever he wants to you,
let him love you, even though it hurts.

abdicate

You give up love for sex
because there had been so many years
without it. The sex a surprise,
the force of it so strong
you are left speechless.
When had you settled for so little?
When had you decided it didn't matter?

Everything about him a surprise—
the first night, he touched your back
and it felt like confirmation of desire.
In bed, he told you he wanted you to come,
his face between your legs,
and you froze, this want never so clear before,
your pleasure his only desire.
How had you missed this for so many years?

Later, he puts his arms around you
and you tense for a moment,
skeptical of affection,
until he kisses the back of your neck,
pulls you closer still as though he wants
no space at all between you,
and something in you relaxes,
all the tensions in your body melting.
You don't trust love, you don't trust joy,
but somehow, you feel it.

pulse

You call me only moments after leaving my house
to tell me there is snow on the highway—
Snow! you say, the surprise clear and sweet in your voice.
It's barely November,
and we are used to months of rain only.

I imagine the slush of it on the side of the road,
the icy crystals sparkling under street lights
as you drive, the hour-long commute home stretching
like so much sleep,
the few hours you'll have before you are back at work.

You'd spent most of Sunday in my bed,
your arms lazily around me,
your right hand absently rubbing my shoulder,
cupping my breast.
The hours unspooled,
our bodies pressed so close together,
and when you slept, you pulled me still closer,
possessive even then.

You said, *Snow!* and I didn't know how to respond,
the weather such a mundane notion
when all you really wanted was to hear my voice,
to hear me say, *Snow?*
and, *Be safe,*
just to listen to me breathe,
maybe wishing yourself back in my bed,
your hand on the pulse in my throat,
as, outside, the snow continued to fall,
as weightless as my heart.

acknowledgements

Some of these poems appeared in previous publications, sometimes in slightly different forms. Thank you to the editors, and to literary magazines for showcasing poetry. We all need more poetry in our lives.

"crushed candy" won 1st Place in *Room Magazine*'s Short Form Contest, 2017.
"safe as houses" received Editors' Choice in *CV2*'s 2-Day Poem, 2017.
"one set of tracks" appeared in *Grain*.
"Room 502" appeared in *Grain*.
"scatter" appeared in *Event*.
"turns to will" appeared in *Event*.
"reckless" appeared in *This Magazine*.
"cherry popsicles" appeared in *This Magazine*.
"manmade" appeared in *This Magazine*.

"unveiled", "Operation Persistence", "this is the last time", "sours", and "precognition" were all written during participation in *CV2*'s 2-Day Poem Contest, in which you must use ten assigned (and maddening) words. See if you can tell which words are those ones.

Thank you to everyone at Book*hug Press, particularly Jay and Hazel Millar—dream publishing house for *Reckless*. Thank you to Britt Landry, Michel Vrana, and Stuart Ross for their care with this collection. Huge thank-you to my editor, Carolyn Smart, for all her thoughtful, incisive, and absolutely right edits to the manuscript. Working with you was perfection.

These poems were written over a particularly difficult time in my life, and I would not have gotten through it without the love, support, and bad-assery of the women I am blessed to know.

Thank you to Amy Read, Allyson Gonzalez, Jenn Prodanuk, Kristine (Keek to me always) Waddell, Sara Forte, Tara Mulldoon, Erin Byrne, Jenn Chandi, Christine (Cricket to me always) Homfeld, Nicole (Nicky to me always) Schroeder, Stacy Ewing, Karen Selesky, Michelle Superle, and Jackie Friesen. My love for you knows no bounds.

None of this would have been possible without the lifelong support and limitless love from my parents, Bob and Lesley MacPherson. I won the lottery with you.

To Jen Sookfong Lee for reading all my horrible first drafts, for always listening and never judging, and for making me laugh even when I was crying. For Serina Townsley for…well everything. For all the years, all the memories, and for being the closest thing I have to a sister.

To all the students who inspired and awed me in their bravery, their optimism, and their joy when putting words on a page. I look forward to buying your books one day. I miss you daily.

And finally, and mostly, and always, to Nora. I'm speechless seeing the person you have become, and I am so proud to be able to say I am your mum. You are the best thing I have ever done, and everything I do is forever for you. Also, maybe skip some of these poems, okay?

about the author

ANDREA MACPHERSON is the author of four poetry collections and three novels. She has been shortlisted for the Ethel Wilson Fiction Prize, longlisted for the ReLit Award, and selected for CBC Canada Reads: People's Choice. Andrea holds an MFA in creative writing from the University of British Columbia, is the former editor of *Prism International*, and has taught creative writing and literature at a number of universities. She lives in Cloverdale, BC, with her daughter.

colophon

Manufactured as the first edition of
Reckless
in the fall of 2025 by Book*hug Press

Edited for the press by Carolyn Smart
Copy-edited by Stuart Ross
Proofread by Britt Landry
Type + design by Jay Millar
Cover by Michel Vrana

Printed in Canada

bookhugpress.ca